Theos Friends' Program

Theos is a religion and society think tank which seeks t
opinion about the role of faith and belief in society.

We were launched in November 2006 with the suppor
Dr Rowan Williams and the Cardinal Archbishop of Wes
Murphy-O'Connor.

We provide

- high-quality research, reports and publications;
- an extensive events programme;
- news, information and analysis to media companies, parliamentarians and other opinion formers.

We can only do this with your help!

Theos Friends receive complimentary copies of all Theos publications, invitations to selected events and monthly email bulletins.

Theos Associates receive all the benefits of Friends and in addition are invited to attend an exclusive annual dinner with the Theos Director and team.

If you would like to become a Friend or an Associate, please visit www.theosthinktank.co.uk or detach or photocopy the form below, and send it with a cheque to Theos for the relevant amount. Thank you.

Yes, I would like to help change public opinion!
I enclose a cheque payable to Theos for: ☐ **£60** (Friend) ☐ **£300** (Associate)
Other amount_____

☐ Please send me information on how to give by direct debit

Name_____

Address _____

_____

_____ Postcode _____

Email _____

Tel _____

Theos will use your personal information to keep you updated about its activities. Theos will not pass your details to any third party to be used for marketing activities. If you wish to change the way we communicate with you please phone us on 02078287777. Theos sub-contracts its data processing. Our data processing contractors are bound by the terms of this statement.

Please return this form to:
Theos | 77 Great Peter Street | London | SW1P 2EZ

S: 97711 D: 36701

Theos – clear thinking on religion and society

Theos is a Christian think tank working in the area of religion, politics and society. We aim to inform debate around questions of faith and secularism and the related subjects of values and identity. We were launched in November 2006, and our first report *'Doing God': a Future for Faith in the Public Square,* written by Nick Spencer, examined the reasons why faith will play an increasingly significant role in public life.

what Theos stands for

In our post-secular age, interest in spirituality is increasing across western culture. We believe that it is impossible to understand the modern world without an understanding of religion. We also believe that much of the debate about the role and place of religion has been unnecessarily emotive and ill-informed. We reject the notion of any possible 'neutral' perspective on these issues.

what Theos works on

Theos conducts research, publishes reports and runs debates, seminars and lectures on the intersection of religion, politics and society in the contemporary world. We also provide regular comment for print and broadcast media. Research areas include religion in relation to public services, the constitution, law, the economy, pluralism and education.

what Theos provides

In addition to our independently driven work, Theos provides research, analysis and advice to individuals and organisations across the private, public and not-for-profit sectors. The Theos team have extensive experience in quantitative, qualitative and ethnographic research and consultancy. For more information about Theos Consultancy contact the team at hello@theosthinktank.co.uk.

what Theos believes

Theos was launched with the support of the Archbishop of Canterbury and the Cardinal Archbishop of Westminster, but it is independent of any particular denomination. We are an ecumenical Christian organisation, committed to the belief that religion in general and Christianity in particular has much to offer for the common good of society as a whole. We are committed to the traditional creeds of the Christian faith and draw on social and political thought from a wide range of theological traditions. We also work with many non-Christian and non-religious individuals and organisations.

"Speaking Up" – Defending and Delivering Access to Justice Today

Andrew Caplen and David McIlroy

Acknowledgement

We would like to register our thanks to Tim and Lorna Lawson-Cruttenden who very kindly contributed towards the cost of this project.

Published by Theos in 2015
© Theos

ISBN 978-0-9574743-7-6

Theos
Licence Department
77 Great Peter Street
London
SW1P 2EZ

T 020 7828 7777
E hello@theosthinktank.co.uk
www.theosthinktank.co.uk

contents

"Speaking Up" – *Defending and Delivering Access to Justice Today* is a timely reminder to Christians both of the importance to our faith of justice, and of the particular responsibility upon Christians to advocate on behalf of those who do not have a voice. Themes of justice and advocacy are a thread running through the Old and New Testaments, as the God of justice encourages His people to be people of justice; as God, who sees and loves the poor and marginalised, encourages His people to care for and to speak out for the poor and those whose voice is not heard.

Our criminal justice system is rooted firmly within and shaped by the Christian inheritance of our land. As Christians we share a commitment to justice and, as part of that, to advocacy on behalf of the poor, marginalised and voiceless. We are, therefore, concerned about many of the recent changes to Legal Aid and the impact upon some of those who most need someone to advocate for them. We exhort individual Christians and churches to respond to these changes in the provision of advocacy and to consider justice as being just as integral to mission and the coming of God's kingdom as is serving the poor, visiting the lonely, teaching the young, healing the sick, and accompanying the dying.

We also call upon all political parties to take seriously the concerns about the impact of changes to Legal Aid upon the government's obligation to provide access to fair and affordable justice. We look to all political parties to outline how they will ensure this access to justice given the financial constraints we face and the changes to access to justice that that have already taken place. For all its real importance, we recognise that Christians advocating for those who are poor, marginalised and voiceless can only be part of the response to concerns about the provision of justice and advocacy for all and that, ultimately, as this report argues, the state has a binding duty to ensure that justice is made available to all.

Dr Andrew Bradstock, Joint Public Issues Team of the Baptist, Methodist and United Reformed Churches
Dr Helen Cameron, Head of Public Affairs, Salvation Army
Dr Dave Landrum, Director of Advocacy, Evangelical Alliance
Rt Revd James Langstaff, the Bishop of Rochester and Bishop to Prisons
Rt Revd Richard Moth, Catholic Bishop of the Forces and liaison Bishop for Prisons
Dr R. David Muir, Co-chair, National Church Leaders Forum, Director of Faith in Britain

executive summary

Christianity places singular emphasis on the rule of law. In particular, it stresses equality before the law, universality of access, the need for legal advocacy, and the impartial administration of justice as being essential to a just society. Providing effective, accessible, universal justice is a fundamental task of government.

Access to justice requires judges who can be trusted to act with integrity, courts that work efficiently, and lawyers who are honest, competent, accessible and affordable. Recent reforms make it less likely that affordable, accessible legal representation will be available in all cases where it is needed.

The result of recent changes is that legal aid is only available in a very small category of clinical negligence cases, and is no longer available in most divorce cases or cases about contact between parents and children with whom they no longer live. Further, legal aid is no longer available in most housing law, employment, debt, immigration, education, and welfare benefit cases. These changes directly affect the life-chances of some of the most vulnerable in our society. The justification advanced by government for these changes is a financial one.

The provision of *pro bono*, not for profit and affordable legal assistance is imperative to redress the impact of the cuts in legal aid – but it is highly unlikely that such services will be able to fill the black hole in access to justice which has been created.

The effect of the recent changes is likely to affect adversely the most disadvantaged in our society. In the longer term it threatens social cohesion, accountability of public bodies and powerful private individuals, and the rule of law. A welfare state is not a substitute for a just state.

Access to justice should be high on the priority of the government, the church, the legal profession and the public. The rule of law is at risk if there is anyone in society who cannot get a fair hearing in the courts; the stability of society is under threat when there are "no go" areas whose inhabitants have no access to justice.

Future changes to the law should be subjected to an independent access to justice impact assessment.

introduction

Nothing rankles more in the human heart than a brooding sense of injustice. Illness we can put up with, but injustice makes us want to pull things down. When only the rich can enjoy the law, as a doubtful luxury, and the poor, who need it most, cannot have it because its expense puts it beyond their reach, the threat to the existence of free democracy is not imaginary but very real, because democracy's very life depends upon making the machinery of justice so effective that every citizen shall believe in the benefit of impartiality and fairness.

US Supreme Court Judge Brennan, 1956

The importance of access to justice cannot be underestimated. It is a fundamental corollary of 'the rule of law' because without access to justice the rule of law can be nothing more than just a concept, an ideal. If access to justice is absent, legal rights cannot be exercised and legal obligations cannot be enforced. Nor can public or private bodies be challenged through the courts, or individuals brought to account. Access to justice is essential to a humane, just and civilized society.

This essay focuses on the availability of, and the ability to obtain and access, legal advice and assistance within England and Wales, partly because it is the legal jurisdiction in which the authors have experience, and partly because the recent changes in this area have had a marked, and worsening, detrimental effect.

Access to justice should be a primary and fundamental Christian concern.

It seeks to argue that the concept of access to justice has deep roots within the tradition of Christian biblical and theological reflection. Access to justice should be a primary and fundamental Christian concern. Thus, notwithstanding the necessary jurisdictional focus on England and Wales, we hope that our underlying arguments and conclusions will translate into other jurisdictions and other times.

Some may consider that our focus on a Christian 'retrieval' of access to justice is not a priority for contemporary Christians. It is certainly true that the most high profile Christian legal activity in recent years within this country has had a somewhat different emphasis.

It is not the purpose of this essay to adjudicate on whether the attempts to protect and sometimes extend the rights of a particular section of the Christian community have tarnished or bolstered the public perception of the Christian message. We do, however, want to suggest that it is not the primary call upon the Church so far as the area of law and legal rights is concerned.

Rather, our view is that the proper Christian focus is on the rights and liberties of others. "Speak up for those who cannot speak for themselves, for the rights of all who are destitute," as the book of Proverbs puts it. "Speak up and judge fairly; defend the rights of the poor and needy."[1] We consider this to be the correct legal priority for the Christian community: to influence for the better society's general understanding of the meaning and importance of justice. At the present time when Legal Aid has been and is being continually cut and, in respect of some types of case, abolished, this entails ensuring that all those who live in England and Wales have access to justice and are therefore able to enjoy the benefits of the rule of law.

There seems little doubt that access to justice in England and Wales is at a crossroads. Successive administrations have either cut funding or removed the scope of legal matters covered by the state-funded Legal Aid scheme. The reason for this is generally claimed to be financial constraints, although sometimes other political considerations have been factors.

At the same time, the legal services market has been undergoing its equivalent of a "big bang" following the enactment of the 2007 Legal Services Act, allowing for the first time, outside investment in law firms and the creation of new types of legal business models known as Alternative Business Structures. This statutory framework rightly sees access to justice as being a regulatory objective, to be taken into account by front-line legal regulators. However, is there a danger of this objective being interpreted as a need to provide different legal services outlets with an emphasis on competition rather than affordable – and if appropriate free or state-funded – legal advice and assistance?

Could it be that access to justice is in danger of becoming a concept more than a reality? Access to justice is generally acknowledged as being a fundamental human right, but is it one that is honoured more in words than in practice? Has it become something to which we pay lip-service, something that is claimed by many and yet available only to few? And should the Church have both a role and a voice, through its traditions, teaching and influence, in contributing to what is surely a vital debate?

This essay has two main parts. The first argues that access to justice is a major concern in the Christian scriptures and that, accordingly, it should be so for Christians. While recent years have seen the emergence of 'justice missions' abroad, there has not been much awareness of the issues in England and Wales. This is largely because failures of justice in the domestic sphere tend, mercifully, to be much rarer and much less severe than they are in various other jurisdictions round the world but, the essay argues, we should not be complacent.

This leads on to the second part, which considers successive governments' attitudes towards the Legal Aid system. While recognising the need to save money in fiscally-straitened times, the essay argues that such policies will inevitably diminish the availability of access to justice, particularly among those that are liable to need it most. Without wishing in any way to be alarmist, it stresses that one of the primary functions of government is to ensure justice is done within (and, as far as is possible, beyond) its territorial boundaries, and that removing or limiting the funds available for those who cannot otherwise afford representation may erode this.

A brief conclusion recaps the arguments and lays challenges before all three relevant parties: Christians should focus more on justice for all, to speak up for those who cannot speak for themselves; the legal profession should take seriously its collective responsibility to make legal services available to those least likely to be able to obtain them under their own steam; and the government and opposition parties should reconsider their policies of restricting and cutting Legal Aid in the light of their impact on the most vulnerable and the damage they risk causing to the rule of law.

introduction references

1   Proverbs 31:8–9 (NIV). All biblical references in this essay are from the New International
     Version unless otherwise stated.

the Bible's concern for justice

In the last half-century or so, the Bible's concern for justice has been an inspiration for Christians from liberation theologians to Jubilee 2000 debt campaigners. Justice has been affirmed as central to the character of God and to the message of both the Hebrew Bible (which Christians usually refer to as the Old Testament) and the New Testament. However, for all the focus on the Bible's teaching about what justice is, there has been less reflection on what has to happen for justice to be done.

This is not an essay about how a utopia can be constructed from the biblical materials, nor does it take a particular biblical theme and make it the centrepiece of a social vision. Instead, its focus is on what the Bible says about the rule of law and, specifically, about how important it is that everyone in a society should have access to justice. Justice according to law may not be perfect justice, but it is indispensable. In particular, the biblical material we examine – necessarily briefly – in this first part of the essay stresses four key points: (1) the need for justice to be administered impartially and equally; (2) the need to ensure universal access to justice; (3) the recognition of how differentials in power and economic imbalances erode both of the above; and (4) the need for advocacy to enable justice to be delivered. These emphases make access to justice a major priority for Christians, and for all people concerned about the future of our society.

justice in the Hebrew Bible

the Hebrew Bible expresses a strong concern for justice

The writer of *The Crucible*, the Jewish playwright Arthur Miller, once said, "We are the people of the Book, and the Book means justice."[1] It is undeniable that two of the principal concerns of the Hebrew Bible are the justice of God and the reflection of God's justice on earth. Israel's foundation as a nation was centred on two events: the just action of God in delivering a people from slavery in Egypt, and Moses giving a law to that people at Mount Sinai so that they might enjoy just relations with one another in the Promised Land.

Although there are features of the Law of Moses which seem strange or even offensive to modern readers, it was revolutionary by comparison with the laws of the surrounding nations. In many ancient legal systems, different rules applied to different categories of person. In contrast, the Law of Moses applied equally to persons of all classes: there was one standard for both the rich the and poor. The same rules also applied both to Israelite citizens and to immigrants.[2] In Deuteronomy 1:16 Moses tells the judges he commissions that they should "judge righteously whether the case is between brother Israelites or between one of them and a foreigner."

Even the king was not above the law. This is in stark contrast to Egypt and the Mesopotamian empires where the king was regarded as the representative of the gods, if not a god himself. In Israelite society, God was and always remains the true king and the human king only his vassal. This meant that the king could be held accountable to God and, crucially, to the nation for his faithfulness in applying the law.

In order to be faithful to the law, the king had to discharge his key responsibility of dispensing justice.[3] This meant both convicting the guilty and acquitting the innocent.[4] King David is praised because he did what was just and right for all his people.[5] When David's son, Absalom rebels against him, he prepares the ground by asserting that he will provide justice where his father has failed to do so.[6] The wisdom of David's chosen successor, Solomon, is demonstrated by his judgment in the case of two prostitutes who are arguing about which one of them is the mother of a dead child and which one the mother of the live child.[7]

One of the later prophets, Zechariah, surveys the decline and fall of the kingdoms of Israel and Judah and attributes it to oppression and the failure to administer justice and to show mercy and compassion.[8] In particular, he highlights the way in which the most vulnerable in society have been oppressed. In the patriarchal culture of Bronze and Iron Age Israel, to be without the protection of a strong male with status in the community was to be exposed both economically and socially. Hence it was the widow (who had lost the protection of her husband), the orphan (who had lost the protection of his or her parents), and the immigrant (who was separated geographically from kinship group) who were at the greatest risk of being the victims of injustice or natural tragedies.

bribery and corruption as enemies of justice

A major theme of the Hebrew Scriptures is the condemnation of bribery. At first sight this appears trite. It would be hard to offer a serious defence of bribery. Nonetheless, simply because something is morally indefensible, that doesn't mean it is rare or unusual. Bribery is constant temptation and a danger for any society.

Its consequences are deleterious. First, bribery distorts outcomes in the legal system by encouraging judges to accept false testimony. A judge who accepts bribes perverts the course of justice and renders unjust verdicts instead of just ones.[9] Second, bribery changes the nature of a legal system: a legal system in which bribes are routinely taken is no longer one that is concerned about right and wrong; instead the answers given by the courts are available to the highest bidder. Law is no longer about justice; it is simply a reflection of pre-existing economic power. When judges can be bought, justice is up for sale and you'd better have enough money to be able to pay for it.

In a system where the rich can buy their way out of liability for their wrongful and illegal actions, the poor no longer enjoy the effective protection of the rule of law.[10] The writers of the book of Proverbs condemn such a situation because the result is that the poor are treated as being worth less than the rich. Since God is the loving creator of both the rich and the poor alike,[11] oppression of the poor is nothing other than an expression of contempt for God himself.[12] As David Cameron acknowledged in his speech to celebrate the 400th anniversary of the King James Bible, the idea that God created human beings, all human beings, in God's own image, was a game changer for the cause of human dignity and equality.[13]

differentials in riches and power as obstacles to justice[14]

Our reflections on bribery have shown that bribery is an egregious example of the extent to which differentials in wealth and power can lead to injustice in the hands of those willing to be corrupted. The prophet Micah expressed the point as well as anyone: "the *ruler* demands gifts, the *judge* accepts bribes, the *powerful* dictate what they desire – they all conspire together."[15]

A variety of recent stories – from celebrity sex scandals, to fraudulent expense claims by politicians and claims of mis-selling by the banks – have re-emphasised that power differentials carry with them the potential for abuse. The problem of the potential for power differentials to result in abuse is exacerbated when the weak have no means of exposing the unjust behaviour or of obtaining redress. Jimmy Saville was able to continue committing sex crimes for as long as he did because the voice of the victims was never listened to.

There is within the Law of Moses a series of measures that were designed to mitigate the extent of power differentials and, through mechanisms like debt forgiveness and the year of Jubilee, to reset them periodically. Even where there is no injustice involved in their respective states, Proverbs 22:7 points out that "the rich rule over the poor, and the borrower is servant to the lender." Financial inequality creates an imbalance of power which is capable of being abused.

The poor are vulnerable simply because they are poor. Rather than conniving in the oppression of the poor by the rich, the courts should act as a counter-balance to it.[16] Therefore, the writers of Proverbs recognise that in order to achieve impartial justice the judges must pay special attention to the claims of the poor.[17] This concern for the poor does not reflect some sentimental view on behalf of these ancient Hebrew writers that the rich are always wicked and that the poor are always in the right. To find for the poor woman simply because she is poor would be to distort justice just as much as to find against her because of her poverty.[18] Leviticus 19:15 warns, "do not pervert justice; do not show partiality to the poor or favouritism to the great, but judge your neighbour fairly."[19]

providing effective justice for all is a key responsibility of rulers

The Hebrew Scriptures see the administration of justice as the most important responsibility of rulers in home affairs.[20] Welfare and health care provision, such as it was, was left to the extended family. Central government's role focused on justice and defence. The link between justice and defence was that both were seen in terms of defending the right and delivering people from oppression.

The Hebrew Bible is concerned to a surprising extent with the accessibility of justice and the availability of means of accountability.

The importance of the king's role in providing justice is clearly seen in the comparison which the book of Jeremiah makes between, on the one hand, Shallum (Jehoahaz) and Jehoiakim, and on the other hand, their father, Josiah. Josiah is commended because, "he did what was right and just, so all went well with him. He defended the cause of the poor and needy, and so all went well. Is that not what it means to know me?"[21] Instead, the motivation of his sons' rule was a desire to build expensive cedar-lined palaces, paid for with the profits from dishonest gain, oppression, extortion, and the shedding of innocent blood.[22] Shallum and Jehoiakim are urged to imitate their father's example, to "do what is just and right. Rescue from the hand of his oppressor the one who has been robbed. Do no wrong or violence to the alien, the fatherless or the widow, and do not shed innocent blood in this place."[23]

The concerns of the Hebrew Scriptures about the legal system go beyond a condemnation of bribery and warnings that the poor should be treated fairly in the courtroom. The Hebrew Bible is concerned to a surprising extent with the *accessibility* of justice and the availability of means of accountability. We are not offered a one-size-fits-all solution but instead a variety of responses to changing social situations.

If one person killed another, the killer was at risk of a revenge attack by the dead person's relatives. The Law of Moses provided that the killer could flee to a City of Refuge where the killer's case would be tried and where the killer would be given asylum if the death was found to have been manslaughter rather than murder. However, because Israel occupied more territory than had originally been anticipated, the number of Cities of Refuge was increased from three to six so that there would always be a venue within easy range where the question "was it murder or was it manslaughter?" could be determined.

Because maintaining justice was seen as a key responsibility of the ruler it was not one which he could wholly delegate. But neither was it possible for a ruler to attempt to resolve all disputes himself. Moses is commended for taking his father-in-law's advice to appoint enough judges so that all disputes could be heard and much later, in the kingdom of Judah, Jehoshaphat is praised for his reforms of the judicial system.[24]

One feature of the Hebrew Bible's approach to justice which is important for the New Testament is the association between justice and deliverance. In the book of Judges, most of what the 'judges' do is not judicial. Only in rare instances, most notably Deborah, are the 'judges' depicted as deciding cases.[25] Instead, the famous stories about Gideon, Samson and the others show them 'judging' by delivering Israel from oppression and injustice. Justice in the courtroom is then also understood in terms of deliverance. By giving judgment for the claimant who is in the right, the king is seen as delivering her from the continued injustice of being deprived of her rights by the defendant who is in the wrong. In the contrary case, by giving judgment for the defendant who is in the right, the king is seen as delivering him from the unjust accusation brought by the claimant who is in the wrong.

To be denied justice is to be prevented from participating in society as a valued and equal member. In its focus on the importance of justice, the Hebrew Bible reveals how a lack of access to justice is a key factor in the persistence of an underclass whose opportunities are limited and whose status is demeaned. Therefore, the king's justice would defend the afflicted, protect the children of the needy, and crush the oppressor.[26] But a concern that the poor get justice is not the sole preserve of the king, according to Proverbs 29:7 it is a dividing line between the just and the wicked.

advocacy and the Hebrew bible

We have suggested so far that the Hebrew Bible is resolutely opposed to a state of affairs in which favourable outcomes in the courtroom are available to the highest bidder and in which the rich are immune from being held accountable by the law. We also find a repeated insistence that rulers are responsible for ensuring that justice is accessible to all, and that justice is administered impartially. As a result, justice and the rule of law exist just as much for the protection of the poor and the vulnerable as they do for the rich and the powerful. We turn in this section to consider how the Hebrew Scriptures see the role of advocacy in securing justice.

Abraham and Moses as advocates

The biblical story of advocacy begins in a surprising place, with the tale of the destruction of the cities of the plain, Sodom and Gomorrah. The moral of this story is more complex than is often recognised, with the book of Ezekiel attributing the judgment on the cities to their arrogance, greed and indifference to the poor and the needy rather than just their sexual practices.[27] It is what happened before the destruction of the cities which is important for present purposes.

In Genesis chapter 13, Abraham and his nephew Lot had parted company. Lot had chosen to live in the plain while Abraham had remained in the hill country. In Genesis 18, Abraham receives three mysterious visitors. Abraham is told that God is about to conduct an on-site inspection of Sodom and Gomorrah and that if it turns out that the state of the cities is as bad as has been reported, then they will be destroyed.[28] Abraham's response is not to congratulate himself on his decision to stay away from the wicked cities but instead to ask God to reconsider. He suggests that God should withhold his judgment of destruction if there are 50 just people within the cities. Having persuaded God on that point, he then talks God down to 45, then 40, then 30, then 20 and finally ten. God agrees that even if only ten just people can be found in the cities of the plain, then their destruction will be forestalled. What we see in that story is an early example of the importance of advocacy, the way in which someone from outside the situation, who is entitled to speak to the decision-maker, can have a real effect on the criteria applied.

Another major figure in the Hebrew Bible who acted as an advocate was Moses. After his encounter at the burning bush, Moses returned to Egypt to negotiate with Pharaoh on behalf of the Hebrew slaves. Later, whilst Moses was on Mount Sinai the people disobeyed God. Moses interceded on behalf of the people, asking that God would forgive their sin and would not abandon them.[29]

the prophets as advocates, reminding the rulers and the powerful of their responsibilities towards the poor

Both Abraham and Moses acted as advocates. Advocacy remains an important role throughout the Hebrew Bible. It was a central aspect of the calling of the prophets. Although we tend to focus on their predictions about the future, the primary responsibility of all the prophets was to speak God's word for now to the rulers and to the people.[30] A major part of the prophets' message was that rulers were both oppressing the people directly and failing to address injustices by others which they ought to have redressed.[31]

On occasion, this role involved the prophet confronting the king directly. Nathan confronted David over his adultery with Bathsheba and murder of her husband.[32] Elijah denounced Ahab for killing Naboth and seizing his land in defiance of the rules on landholding set down in the law of Moses.[33]

Later prophets continued to make injustice a priority even at times when it might be expected that they would have bigger fish to fry. In Jeremiah's time, Judah was invaded and the city of Jerusalem was besieged. Even in this context, Jeremiah's message to the royal house of Judah was: "this is what the Lord says: 'Administer justice every morning; rescue from the hand of his oppressor the one who has been robbed...' "[34]

the lack of an advocate as an enemy of justice

Advocacy is a skill. It requires the capacity to assimilate and organise information, to identify which features of a situation are important and which are not, and the ability to be able to tell a coherent story. Good advocacy helps a judge to do justice because the advocate can help the judge to see the real issues in the case and so to discern who is in the right and who is in the wrong. An advocate represents someone. They present a case in a structured way so that those deciding can get the heart of the problem and can see the wood for the trees.

The importance of representation is stressed by the major prophets Isaiah and Jeremiah. At the very beginning of the book of Isaiah, the prophet says, "learn to do right; seek justice. Defend the oppressed. Take up the cause of the fatherless; plead the case of the widow."[35] The tasks of an advocate – defending, pleading, arguing for a cause – are all presented by Isaiah as aspects of what it means to seek justice and to do right.

Jeremiah declares that God's judgment is coming on the nation of Judah because "their evil deeds have no limit; they do not plead the case of the fatherless to win it, they do not defend the rights of the poor."[36] Lack of concern for the poor and the orphaned are presented as offensive to God and as leading to society's destruction.

Esther as an advocate, intervening with King Xerxes

So far we have seen that Abraham and Moses took on the role of advocates, and that the prophets spoke out against injustice on behalf of the vulnerable and the poor. We have discovered that the Hebrew Scriptures regarded speaking out on behalf of another as an important role which was needed in order to prevent oppression of the vulnerable. Within the Hebrew Scriptures themselves this theme comes to a climax in the book of Esther.

Esther was a Jewish girl who had become the wife of the Persian emperor, King Xerxes, because she won a beauty contest held to find a replacement for his previous queen, Vashti. Vashti had fallen out of favour with Xerxes because she had refused to parade her beauty before the people and the nobles when the king requested her to do so.[37] The clear impression the text gives of Xerxes is that he was a volatile and unstable man, capable of violent mood-swings, and to be approached with great care.

Haman, the chief minister of Xerxes, had managed to secure from the king an order that the Jews be annihilated.[38] Esther's uncle became aware of this intended genocide and contacted Esther to ask her to help. Esther could have kept quiet about her Jewish identity and relied on her relationship to the king to keep her beyond Haman's reach. Instead, she resolved to risk her own life by going to see King Xerxes and asking him to spare the life of her people.[39] Esther's advocacy was successful, Haman was hanged upon his own gallows and the plot was averted. Esther's actions and the deliverance they secured are still celebrated today as the Jewish festival of Purim.

the need for advocacy in the courtroom

In the courtroom, the poor are particularly exposed to the risk of injustice if they have no-one to act on their behalf, no-one who can tell their story for them in a way that is compelling and easy to grasp. The Hebrew Bible addresses this in two ways. As we have already seen, the Law of Moses specifically urges judges not to deny justice to poor people in their lawsuits.[40] Judges need to take the time and make the effort to listen to those who are forced to represent themselves. However, the book of Proverbs also calls on others to intervene, to act as advocates on behalf of those whose voice would otherwise not be heard. In the words of Proverbs 31:8–9, which has become a motto for more than one Christian organisation engaged in advocacy, we should "speak up for those who cannot speak for themselves, for the rights of all who are destitute. Speak up and judge fairly; defend the rights of the poor and needy."

the God of justice wants to see justice done on earth

The importance of justice is not accidental but fundamental to the Hebrew Bible. It is fundamental because the authors of the Law, the Prophets and the Writings saw justice as a central characteristic of God. YHWH is the God of Justice. God is the great king who will do justice.[41]

Throughout the Hebrew Bible there is a profound wrestling with the question: is God just? The unequivocal answer given is that, notwithstanding the injustice seen on earth, God is just, indeed justice is fundamental to God's character. God's love of justice and hatred of injustice are a recurrent theme. "Let him who boasts boast about this," Jeremiah 9:24 declares, "that he understands and knows me, that I am the Lord, who exercises kindness, justice and righteousness on earth, for in these I delight."[42]

This belief that God is just leads the Psalmist to proclaim, "the Lord is a refuge for the oppressed… He does not ignore the cry of the afflicted."[43] Given God's commitment to justice, and given the continuing presence of manifest injustice on earth, there is an increasing expectation by the prophets that God will intervene within history to right wrongs. The prophet Isaiah declares, "the Lord is our judge, the Lord is our lawgiver, the Lord is our king, it is he who will save us."[44] The Hebrew Scriptures raise the question: if God is just, what is God going to do to bring about justice on earth, and when and how is God going to do it? The Christian answer is that God's decisive intervention occurred in the person of Jesus Christ.

God and justice in the New Testament

There is a widespread perception that justice is not a major theme in the New Testament. The existence of Israel and Judah as states in Old Testament times and the fact that the New Testament says relatively little about government[45] can point to the erroneous conclusion that whereas the Old Testament is very much concerned with justice on earth, the New Testament focuses instead on the final Day of Judgment.

This is a serious misreading. It is, however, one which is encouraged by the tendency of English versions of the Bible to use the word "righteousness" where both the original Greek and some modern languages such as French would use the word "justice".

Jesus is justice personified

Christians recognize Jesus of Nazareth to be the fulfilment of the hopes expressed in the Hebrew Bible. If, as we have seen, prominent amongst these was the hope that God would bring about justice on earth, then, if Christianity's claims about Jesus are sustainable, one would expect to find that Jesus did answer the hope for God's justice in some way.

The classic passage in which Jesus is taken to be making such a claim is Luke 4:16–21, which has been called 'the Nazareth manifesto'. In that passage, Jesus reads from Isaiah 61:1–2 which talks about a figure anointed to preach good news to the poor, to proclaim freedom for the prisoners, recovery of sight for the blind, and release for the oppressed. He then sits down after reading and announces that "Today this scripture is fulfilled in your hearing."

In the last couple of hundred years there has been a tendency to treat Jesus' mission as being one which was exclusively concerned with people's spiritual or psychological condition. Christianity is about finding peace with oneself, with the world and with God. That is not how his original hearers would have taken it. There were some within their community who were suffering from real poverty, because of the precarious nature of their subsistence existence or because of Roman taxes. There were those who were unjustly imprisoned, the victims of the law and order policies of the occupying powers. There were others afflicted by physical blindness and many affected by the oppressive power structures which collaborated and competed in extortion and subjection of the people. The issues to which Jesus spoke were issues of justice, including economic justice.[46] They were issues raised by a man who claimed to be God's chosen Messiah, "living among the broken and lost of an occupied and humiliated people."[47]

Nor is the Nazareth Manifesto a one-off set-piece without any follow-up. In the Sermon on the Mount, Jesus declared, "Blessed are those who hunger and thirst for justice, for they will be filled".[48] He told his followers to seek first God and God's justice[49] and saved his harshest words for the Pharisees who claimed great knowledge of God but neglected "the more important matters of God's law: justice, mercy and faithfulness."[50]

It might seem that Jesus' words were not matched by his actions. On one occasion he expressly declined to act as a judge in an inheritance dispute.[51] The picture changes, however, when justice is understood as deliverance. From that perspective, the healings which Jesus performed and the forgiveness which Jesus offered are acts of justice, delivering people from the oppression of ill-health and guilt. His miraculous provision of food is symbolic of a just society in which everyone has their fair share. In his life, Jesus demonstrates that justice is about much more than what goes on in the legal process. The concepts of advocacy and judgment are key to understanding Christianity's claims about his death and resurrection.

justice and injustice in the death and resurrection of Jesus

The relationship between God's justice and human legal systems comes to a climax in the events of the first Easter. Jesus was tried at night by the chief priests in a secret religious court and then handed over to the Roman authorities for execution. Pontius Pilate, the Roman governor, found Jesus innocent of any crimes against Roman law, but nonetheless gave the crowd the option of having a rebel, Barabbas, released instead. Christian theology sees that switch as a demonstration of the greater truth that Jesus, the innocent one, has died on behalf of guilty humanity. The death of Jesus is the most extreme form of representation imaginable in which the advocate not only acts on behalf of the litigant but pays his penalty too.

The echoes of the courtroom in the Easter story do not end with Good Friday. From Friday afternoon until Sunday morning, the verdict hangs in the balance: how will God respond to the execution of Jesus? Jesus now stands in the place of the one who has been oppressed, denied his rights and tortured to death. The question raised by the Hebrew Scriptures comes to a focal point: in the final analysis, will God do justice and deliver the one who has become vulnerable and the victim of violence?

The message of the empty tomb and of the resurrection appearances is that God will act justly, that God has overturned the verdict of the human courts, and that God has vindicated Jesus and declared him to be just.

The connection between Jesus and justice goes beyond the resurrection. In the midst of his sufferings, Job had called out for someone to be a witness for him in heaven, he had asked for an advocate on high, who could intercede with God on his behalf "as a man pleads for his friend."[52] 1 John 2:1 presents Jesus as having just such a role, not only on behalf of the innocent who are suffering, but also as a defence advocate able to offer a plea on behalf of those who are guilty and sinful. Finally, the New Testament concludes with the book of Revelation, in which Jesus will return again to earth to judge with justice.[53]

The New Testament therefore presents Jesus as the guarantor that: (1) God's judgments are just, (2) God's justice is accessible to all, (3) that human beings have an advocate who will intercede with God on their behalf, and (4) as the Christian church expands beyond ethnic Jews, God's justice is universal.

justice in the remainder of the New Testament

A key question that the early Church had to confront was whether its message was for a select group (either ethnic Jews or those with access to its secret knowledge) or was accessible to all. Its conclusion by the end of the first century was that the good news was available to all without distinction. In the letter to the Romans, Paul also worked through the question of God's justice and demonstrated how God's justice applies equally to both Jews and non-Jews.[54] In that letter Paul holds in tension his unequivocal assertion that God's justice is equally available to all and his concern for his own people, the Jews. In Romans 9 to 11 we find Paul acting as an advocate pleading with God on their behalf. The themes of universality, accessibility and advocacy are therefore clear in what the New Testament teaches about God's justice – but does the New Testament have anything to say about how these apply to legal systems on earth?

Everyone was not equal under Roman law. Some people were slaves and had few or no rights; others were subjects; only Roman citizens enjoyed a full range of rights. Paul was a Roman citizen and in his interaction with the authorities, we see him asserting his legal rights. At the Roman colony of Philippi, he is stripped, beaten and thrown into prison.[55] The following morning, the magistrates give the order to release him but Paul refuses to leave unless the magistrates publicly escort him and his companion Silas out of the city.[56] Why does he do this? Paul is laying down a marker that Roman citizens who are Christians retain their rights, something that will be important for the protection of the fledging church that he is leaving behind in the Roman colony. Later, Paul defends himself before Festus and insists on his legal right to appeal to the emperor.[57] Paul was prepared to claim the rights which the Roman legal system gave him.

He also used the legal hearings to explain Christianity. He did this not just in the hope of converting his hearers but also so that they might understand that Christianity was not a sect advocating violent revolution but rather one whose adherents should be given the toleration which the Roman Empire already extended to the Jews. Paul's successes in being able to access justice and to advocate in ways that protected other Christians were key factors in the spread of early Christianity. He also sowed the seeds which would eventually undermine the inequalities in status in Roman law, declaring "There is neither Jew nor Greek, slave nor free, male nor female, for you are all one in Christ Jesus."[58] The Christian message, although fitfully applied throughout history, is that justice must not only be accessible to all: it must also be universal.

justice and the Church today

The history of the Church shows a mixed reaction to the Bible's teaching about the importance of justice. The ideas that justice is universal, that it should be accessible to all, and that advocacy is indispensable to its achievement are perhaps most famously exhibited, within the British context, by the efforts of William Wilberforce and the Clapham Sect on behalf of the victims of the slave trade. Hundreds of years before that, however, similar points had been made on behalf of the natives of South America by Bartholome de las Casas, Francisco de Vitoria and Francisco Suárez, though sadly to less effect. Nonetheless, these are still instances of advocacy beyond and outside the courtroom.

The time has surely come for British Christians to take action in two ways. Firstly, to remind government that it has a fundamental responsibility to secure justice, and secondly, to consider urgently ways in which they might, as part of their mission, be involved in assisting with the provision of advice and representation in cases where the government is unwilling or unable to discharge its responsibility.

In the last twenty years, we have seen the development of a number of initiatives where Christian organisations have made it part of their mission to represent people in legal issues, and this is increasingly seen as just as legitimate an activity as medical or educational mission. These initiatives include providing representation to defend the rights of Christians but they go far broader than that. The American charity International Justice Mission operates in a number of countries around the world, prosecuting the perpetrators of human trafficking, investigating cases of slavery and illegal expropriation of land, and exposing horrific sex crimes. It has developed an impressive record of securing just outcomes on behalf of women and children, the poor and the vulnerable, even within legal systems that are far from perfect. In 2010, International Justice Mission rescued 42 slaves, half of whom were children, from a rock quarry in India. In 2014, it saw the slave owner convicted and sentenced to seven years in prison. This was only the sixth conviction under India's anti-slavery laws and the longest sentence ever passed.

Christian charities (such as the UK organisation BMS World Mission) operating in Uganda, Kenya, Mozambique and Rwanda provide legal defence advice to those who cannot afford it, and advice to women on their rights in divorce, custody and inheritance cases, as well as giving the poor access to basic legal education on issues such as protection of land, making wills, and protection of children from abuse. Through legal education they equip people to represent themselves more effectively and they provide para-legals who are able to observe conditions in police stations and prisons and to locate, understand and complete legal paperwork. Their successes include, for example, the release of a Muslim man who spent seven years in prison because he was framed by a neighbour. Many women have also secured a financial settlements and access to their children, simply because someone was prepared to tell them their rights, support them and speak on their behalf.

Initiatives such as these, to which we shall return in the final part of this essay, represent the culmination of half a century during which we have seen the increasing recognition amongst both secular and Christian organisations of the importance of advocacy and effective access to justice as a powerful tool in improving people's life-prospects and in community transformation. The British Government's Department for International Development (DfID) has taken a lead in identifying good governance as one of the key factors in development, in recognition of the fact that, without access to justice and the rule of law, other poverty eradication goals become meaningless, as an individual's personal liberty and property are not secure.[59] Advocacy and effective access to justice are therefore a powerful tools in improving people's life-prospects and in community transformation.

advocacy begins at home?

Despite this recovered recognition of the importance of justice and the value of advocacy in securing it, there remains a certain amount of inconsistency in the attitude of British churches here. Advocacy has, up to now, often been regarded as an issue for overseas mission (if regarded as an issue at all) rather than as a matter for the UK.

Recent changes restricting the availability of Legal Aid indicate that such an assumption is no longer sound. The time has surely come for British Christians to take action in two ways. Firstly, to remind government that it has a fundamental responsibility to secure justice, and that means ensuring that everyone, including the poor, is able to be heard and to obtain their rights. Secondly, to consider urgently ways in which they might, as part of their mission, be involved in assisting with the provision of advice and representation in cases where the government is unwilling or unable to discharge its responsibility. If the voice of the poor and the vulnerable is no longer properly represented, there has to be a serious risk that injustices will occur and that our democratic bedrock of the rule of law will be threatened. The Church should be concerned.

conclusion

> *It is when you have an advocate, someone to intervene on your behalf, that you are not forgotten. No matter how impeccable the laws are on paper, if you don't know how to assert your rights or tell your story, those laws may as well not exist.*

In this chapter we have seen that the Hebrew Bible stresses the responsibility of rulers to secure justice for all, including the poor, the vulnerable, the friendless, and the immigrant. Situations where bribery, inequality or other factors mean that justice can be bought are unequivocally condemned. We have also identified how much emphasis the Hebrew Bible places on the role of the advocate in securing justice. We have traced how the New Testament identifies Jesus as the one who personifies justice, as the one who is our advocate in heaven, and as the one who will judge justly. We have also touched on how some parts of the Church are responding to these biblical themes today in various countries through the provision of advocacy both to prosecute and defend the rights of the vulnerable.

We can conclude from the above that providing effective, accessible, universal justice is a fundamental task of government. In fact, both during the times when the Hebrew Scriptures were written and in the Christian era, the ruler's responsibility for ensuring justice was seen as foundational, whereas there was no suggestion that the ruler should provide universal health care or deliver universal education. For centuries, the key tasks of government centred on courts rather than hospitals and schools.

We can also see how effective justice requires advocacy. One of the historic protections English law provided to those within its jurisdiction was the writ of *habeas corpus*. This enabled someone imprisoned in England to be produced in court, where a public determination would be made as to whether they had been imprisoned lawfully or not. It is when you have an advocate, someone to intervene on your behalf, that you are not forgotten. No matter how impeccable the laws are on paper, if you don't know how to assert your rights or tell your story, those laws may as well not exist.

The rule of law is only effective when all members of society are able to enjoy its protection. This means ensuring that all have access to the courts and all have access to adequate representation. Of course, the cost of providing such representation must be kept within reasonable limits and, of course, the assistance and facilitation provided by the government may properly focus on the most serious cases. Those are matters on which political judgments may differ. However, what must be recognised, when making such decisions is that where access to justice is missing, the life-chances of the worst-off and vulnerable in society deteriorate.

Our survey of Christianity and its roots presents a challenge to government to ensure that the poor have effective access to justice, and that includes having access to affordable legal representation. This also presents a challenge to all members of society – to recognise the risks to our neighbours, to our social fabric, and to our ability to relate to one other on the basis that we are all equal before the law, if the poor are excluded from access to justice – as well as a challenge to Christians themselves. If government is failing or refusing to ensure that people have effective representation, can Christians serve their neighbours by standing in that gap, speaking up for them, especially when they are at their most vulnerable? It is to these challenges that the rest of this essay turns.

chapter 1 – references

1 Sarah Katz, 'Arthur Miller calls for justice', *Jerusalem Post*, 27 June 2003, available on-line at http://www.freerepublic.com/focus/f-news/936820/posts

2 Leviticus 24:22.

3 Baldwin *Commentary on 1 and 2 Samuel* p. 117; Christopher Wright *Living as the People of God* p. 38.

4 See Proverbs 17:15.

5 2 Samuel 8:15.

6 2 Samuel 15:1–6.

7 1 Kings 3.

8 Zechariah 7:8–12.

9 Proverbs 17:23, 17:8 and 21:14

10 Gary A. Haugen and Victor Boutros, *The Locust Effect: Why the End of Poverty requires the End of Violence* (Oxford: OUP, 2014) p. 134.

11 Proverbs 22:2.

12 Proverbs 14:31; 17:5.

13 David Cameron, speech at Christchurch, Oxford, on 16 December 2011, http://www.politicshome.com/uk/article/42180/david_camerons_speech_on_the_king_james_bible.html

14 Proverbs 18:23; Exodus 23:6; Leviticus 19:15.

15 Micah 7:3.

16 Proverbs 22:22–23.

17 Proverbs 21:13.

18 Christopher Wright *Living as the People of God* p. 147.

19 See also Exodus 23:3 and Deuteronomy 1:17.

20 Joseph Blenkinsopp *Wisdom and Law in the Old Testament* p. 2.

21 Jeremiah 22:15b–16.

22 Jeremiah 22:13, 17.

23 Jeremiah 22:2–5.

24 2 Chronicles 19:5–11.

25 Judges 4:5.

26 Psalm 72:4.

27 Ezekiel 16:49.

28 Genesis 18:20–21.

29 Exodus 32:30–33.

30 Birch, Brueggemann, Fretheim and Petersen *A Theological Introduction to the Old Testament* pp. 293–4; Knight *A Christian Theology of the Old Testament* p. 315.

31 Christopher Wright *Living as the People of God p.* 146.

32 2 Samuel 12:1–14.

33 1 Kings 21.

34 Jeremiah 21:12.

35 Isaiah 1:17.

36 Jeremiah 5:28–29.

37 Esther 1:11.

38 Esther 3:13.

39 Esther 8:3.

40 Exodus 23:6.

41 Psalm 103:6.

42 See also Isaiah 61:8.

43 Psalm 9:9, 12. See also Psalm 11; 12:5; Exodus 23:7; Proverbs 6:16–17; 1 Kings 20:31; 2 Kings 6:22; 24:4; Isaiah 59:7; James 5:4.

44 Isaiah 33:22.

45 Romans 13:1–7 being the key exception.

46 cf. Peter Selby, *Grace and Mortgage*.

47 Nick Spencer, *Freedom and Order*, p. 297.

48 Matthew 5:6.

49 Matthew 6:33.

50 Matthew 23:23, also Luke 11:42

51 Luke 12:14.

52 Job 16:19–21.

53 Revelation 19:11.

54 See especially Romans 3.

55 Acts 16:22–23.

56 Acts 16:37–40.

57 Acts 25:8–12.

58 Galatians 3:28.

59 A point explored at book length in Gary A. Haugen and Victor Boutros: *The Locust Effect: Why the End of Poverty Requires the End of Violence* (OUP, 2014).

contemporary concerns for justice

The first part of this essay argued that access to justice was a serious concern of the Christian scriptures and that thus it should be for Christians. It hinted at how justice is increasingly being viewed as a calling for Christians in many countries, but that this has yet to be seen to the same extent in the UK. Part two helps explain why. It begins by looking at the historical background to the provision of Legal Aid services in England and Wales, before taking the story up to date with recent reforms to Legal Aid, and their potential consequences. Throughout, the overarching point is straightforward: we take universal, equitable access to justice for granted at our peril.

the road to Legal Aid

The ability to obtain and afford legal advice, assistance and representation in England and Wales, as in almost all countries, was, for much of our history, the preserve of the wealthy and connected.

The year 2015 is the 800th anniversary of the signing of the Magna Carta, "The Great Charter of the Liberties of England", which Lord Denning once described as "the greatest constitutional document of all times – the foundation of the freedom of the individual against the arbitrary authority of the despot." Magna Carta was, of course, forced upon King John by his barons in an attempt to limit his powers as king and to protect their privileges. It was rather less concerned to define and protect civil liberties than was subsequently imagined. The declaration that no "freeman" could be punished except through the law of the land, for example, did not apply to serfs, whose fate remained in the hands of the lord to whom they were attached. Magna Carta was, however, the first major step in limiting the power of the executive (at that time the king) and in laying the foundation in England of the rule of law.

Succeeding centuries saw the further erosion of the powers of the monarch and the extension of the rights of the individual, such as by virtue of Habeas Corpus, a legal action that requires a person under arrest to be brought before a judge or into court, so ensuring that a prisoner can be released from unlawful detention (that is, detention lacking sufficient cause or evidence), first codified by the Habeas Corpus Act 1679.

Individuals could increasingly expect to receive a court trial, but legal representation in the criminal courts was rare. "Dock Briefs" would sometimes be provided. These were a privilege granted by a trial judge to a prisoner in the dock who was unable to obtain counsel for himself, whereby a barrister from those present in the court could be selected to represent the defendant for a nominal fee. Otherwise, legal advice and assistance for poorer litigants, whether in criminal or civil trials, relied on the goodwill of solicitors and barristers, who could at best provide a limited amount of assistance as they themselves had to earn a living from fee-paying work.

> *Legal advice and assistance for poorer litigants, relied on the goodwill of solicitors and barristers, who could at best provide a limited amount of assistance.*

Until the mid-eighteenth century the criminal courts were, in fact, often devoid of lawyers. Prosecutions were usually pursued by well-respected citizens and defence counsels were almost non-existent. Lawyers did not become a common feature in criminal trials until the latter part of the eighteenth century, and even then almost always only on the side of the prosecution. It was not until 1836 that lawyers were granted the right to address juries on behalf of a defendant, although that itself was only available to those who could afford to employ defence counsel or had been granted the benefit of a Dock Brief.

The Poor Persons Defence Act 1903 allowed magistrates to order payment of legal help for defendants utilising "local funds". However, there were limitations to this. For example, the defendant had to disclose his defence no later than at the hearing when his case was due to be committed for trial. Legal representation for a defendant in a criminal trial remained the exception rather than the norm. The requirement for "early disclosure" was eventually removed by the enactment of the Poor Prisoners Defence Act 1930, which also introduced the concept of an "interests of justice" based merits test and extended the discretion of magistrates in deciding whether or not to grant publicly funded legal help.

Free legal assistance in civil cases continued to rely upon the goodwill of solicitors and barristers. In 1914, a change in the rules allowed a civil litigant of modest means and a strong case to be assigned a lawyer to investigate his case and report to the High Court or the Court of Appeal. The judge then had the discretion as to whether to assign a barrister or a solicitor, drawn from a list of volunteers who were willing to work without remuneration.

Legal Aid in England and Wales was finally established by the Legal Aid and Advice Act 1949, as part of the Attlee government's Welfare State reforms after the Second World War and as a result of the recommendations of the Rushcliffe Committee Report of 1945. The Legal Aid scheme created by the 1949 Act was intended to allow litigants of limited means to be able to access legal advice and assistance provided by lawyers from the private sector, to include representation at court hearings. The assistance remained limited at first but the foundations for a modern system of Legal Aid provision had been laid.

the rising cost of Legal Aid

The cost of Legal Aid has increased substantially since the 1949 Act (although it has been falling annually since 2010). It has been suggested that this has been caused by lawyers "milking the system" at the state's expense. Yet during the last twenty years, the rates of pay for various different kinds of Legal Aid have both decreased in actual terms and decreased in real terms because increases in rates (if any) have been below the rate of inflation. During the same period, for a High Street Solicitors' practice (the general means by which Legal Aid services have traditionally been provided) the cost of employing staff has increased substantially, as has that of technology (a cost that twenty years ago would have been minimal), office rents, and business rates.

There are a number of reasons why the Legal Aid budget has expanded so dramatically since the enactment of the Legal Aid and Advice Act in 1949, reasons that can be divided according to whether they pertain to criminal or civil cases.

criminal cases

One key reason for the increase in the cost of Legal Aid in criminal cases lies in who was funding it. Under the Poor Person's Defence Act, magistrates utilised "local funds" (i.e. money from local ratepayers) as the funding source for grants of Legal Aid. Magistrates were, however, generally local people and well aware of local financial pressures. They were consequently often reluctant to allow such funds to be expended in this way. In 1960, however, the Government decided that Legal Aid should be paid for by taxpayers through a national Legal Aid Fund for magistrates' courts and via the Home Office for the higher courts. Not surprisingly, many magistrates became more willing to grant Legal Aid orders following this change to the funding system. The ensuing increase notwithstanding, it is surely right that Legal Aid be provided by the state as it is the state's responsibility to provide access to justice for its citizens, and that the decision whether or not to grant

Legal Aid must be kepy completely separate from the Executive, as in many cases it will be the state that is aligned against the defendant or claimant.

A second reason lies in what constitutes a sufficient call for legal aid. In 1964, Lord Widgery explicitly defined the meaning of "in the interests of justice", the 'test' that had to be passed before a grant of legal representation (i.e. of Legal Aid) could be made by a magistrates' court. His definition was:

a.   that the offence would, if proved, lead to loss of liberty, loss of livelihood or serious damage to the defendant's reputation; or

b.   that the case involved a substantial question of law; or

c.   that the defendant was unable to understand the proceedings or to state his own case due to inadequate English, mental illness, or mental or physical incapacity; or

d.   that the nature of the defence involved tracing and interviewing witnesses, or expert cross-examination of witnesses; or

e.   that it was in the interests of someone other than the defendant that the defendant should be represented.

These criteria remain in existence. They mean that Criminal Legal Aid is by necessity 'demand driven', i.e. the Criminal Legal Aid budget will rise or fall depending upon the number of defendants and cases that fall within Lord Widgery's criteria. There is an inherent tension here, however. Any Government would undoubtedly – and understandably – prefer that the budget available be resources limited.

Third, the 1984 Police and Criminal Evidence Act (PACE) extended the scope of free legal help in criminal proceedings. PACE was the Government's response to the Philips Royal Commission on Criminal Procedure, tasked with reviewing the criminal process from the start of the investigation to the point of trial, following a number of highly publicised cases of intimidation and assault upon suspects at the police station. Whereas previously Legal Aid had been limited to representation in court proceedings, PACE provided for assistance to be made available at police stations during the investigative stage of the criminal process.

A Fairer Deal for Legal Aid, presented to Parliament in 2005 by the then Lord Chancellor Lord Falconer, stated that the Philips Royal Commission had estimated in 1981 that providing free police station advice would only cost around £6 million per year. However, the cost of the police station scheme was £85 million in 1994 and £172 million in 2004–2005, in real terms.

Police station advice has not, to date, been means-tested, meaning that anybody arrested for matters within the scope covered by PACE is entitled to free legal advice (although in some more minor matters this is limited to just telephone assistance rather than actual attendance by a legal representative at the police station). Police station advice should remain on a non means-tested basis – for purely practical reasons, if nothing else. A person arrested on suspicion of an alleged offence is exceptionally unlikely to be in actual possession of sufficient evidence of their means (or lack of them) to prove their entitlement to receive Legal Aid due to lack of those means, or alternatively to be able to provide payment themselves for legal services.

The importance of good quality legal advice at a police station during the investigatory process should not be underestimated. It can lead to earlier guilty pleas benefiting (i) the criminal process by saving costs elsewhere; (ii) witnesses by sparing them the ordeal of testifying; and (iii) defendants themselves by resulting in reduced sentences. Such advice also assists in minimising injustices through, for example, questionable confession statements extracted from accused persons as a result of undue pressure by the police. The presence of legal advisors at a police station both holds the police accountable for their behaviour and generally removes the risk of later suggestions that they behaved inappropriately.

civil cases

The extension of spend on Civil Legal Aid was a result of a number of factors. Firstly, ever more areas of law were covered by the scope of the Legal Aid scheme. Under the original 1949 Act, many of the original Rushcliffe proposals were limited. For example, Civil help was initially restricted to High Court divorce cases following a sharp upturn in applications from returning servicemen and their spouses. Over the years, the areas of law covered increased to include a multitude of matters such as, among others (at the "high water mark" of Legal Aid provision), debt, housing, immigration, personal injury, clinical negligence, welfare benefits, consumer disputes, matrimonial and children matters, and even, in some circumstances, the drafting of simple wills.

Second, the general public has a greater awareness of legal rights. This is very different from a 'blame' or 'compensation' culture. Rather, it is a realisation, through better education and information, that all members of society have legal rights, duties and obligations. This has been associated with the perfectly proper desire to exercise and enforce such legal rights; in effect, a wish by people to access justice themselves.

Third, there is more and more law, and the law is increasingly complex. There is more than a little irony to government complaints about the cost of Legal Aid when a major factor is the increase in the volume and complexity of government legislation. If English law was a set of broad principles applied in a common sense manner, then perhaps at least some litigants would be able to represent themselves adequately. When it has become a complex forest of different layers of European directives, British statutes, departmental regulations and case-law it is little wonder if even the professionals take some time to find their way through it.

Fourth, there is a greater availability of legal services, in large part in response to the factors set out above. The number of lawyers has grown substantially since the Second World War. In the last 30 years alone, the number of solicitors holding a practising certificate has tripled. The number of independent/self-employed barristers has also increased dramatically. This rise in numbers is only marginally linked to the increase in the Legal Aid spend. For example, London's position as a worldwide financial and professional services hub has resulted in a substantial rise in the number of City lawyers. The large rise in home ownership has meant a need for more solicitors practising in the area of residential conveyancing. The increase in the number of lawyers able to advise individual clients does, however, undoubtedly have a link with the increased public awareness of legal issues.

It should be noted that the number of lawyers providing Civil and/or Criminal Legal Aid services has fallen during recent years. Whereas in 1990 most provincial firms of solicitors would have been prepared to take on Legal Aid work, far fewer currently have contracts with the Legal Aid Agency. This is primarily due to the severely decreased financial viability of Legal Aid work coupled with complex (and unpaid) administrative responsibilities. That number has recently been reduced further as a result of the changes to Legal Aid (both in the scope of matters covered by the scheme and decreases in remuneration) as a result of the Legal Aid, Sentencing and Punishment of Offenders Act 2012.

Fifth, there have been marked social and economic changes in society. An increased number of family breakdowns has meant more legal work is necessary to resolve the resulting legal and financial issues. Similarly, consumer redress in respect of faulty workmanship is much more of an issue simply because there are more goods being bought and sold.

Sixth, the complexity of our technological age is also relevant. For example, Data Protection issues were a marginal concern twenty years ago. Today, they constitute a significant and growing issue and appear likely to come more and more to the fore.

Finally, there is an increased public perception of the need for accountability. Again, this is not the same as a blame culture. Rather, it is an appreciation that individuals, companies, public bodies, and the government can and should be held accountable for their actions, ultimately via the court process. This is right and proper, albeit potentially uncomfortable for those being subjected to such challenges.

Between them, these reasons, combined with those outlined above pertaining to criminal cases, have resulted in rising Legal Aid costs and the consequent political determination to trim the legal aid budget.

the restriction of Legal Aid

It is probable that the high-water mark of Legal Aid was attained in the late 1980s. The introduction of police station advice via PACE had taken place a few years earlier. Magistrates' courts had Court Duty schemes where the Court Duty Solicitors were paid by the state. Legal Aid was fairly easily available in criminal trials (albeit subject to the overriding check of Lord Widgery's criteria).

Further, the scope of matters covered by Civil Legal Aid had expanded and was continuing to do so. Payment rates to those lawyers undertaking such work were raised broadly in line with inflation and were at a level close enough to those charged by lawyers undertaking private, i.e. non-Legal Aid, work that the number of lawyers prepared to assist legally-aided clients was proportionately quite high. And, although Civil Legal Aid was means-tested, the financial limits were such that many people on more than just minimal incomes qualified under the scheme, albeit subject to sometimes having to make contributions towards their legal costs.

There had been a growing concern within government at the expansion of a budget that was essentially demand-led rather than resources-limited. The first major attempt to rein in Legal Aid spending occurred whilst Lord Mackay of Clashfern was Lord Chancellor, from 1987 to 1997. When the Labour government was elected in 1997, the Legal Aid budget came under renewed scrutiny. David Blunkett, then Home Secretary, referred to "the fat cats of Legal Aid", a phrase which has unfortunately stuck, while Justice Secretary Jack Straw frequently claimed that England and Wales spent more per head on Legal Aid than any other country in the world.

This comparison was not, perhaps, the fairest. England and Wales have a Common Law legal system based on an adversarial process, where the cost of lawyers is large but the cost of judicial time is relatively small unless a trial takes place. Most European countries have systems based on an inquisitorial process, where the judge plays a far greater role in the management of the case. A proper comparison would have to include the cost to the public purse of both judges and Legal Aid payments to lawyers in each instance.

Moreover, to compare the costs of a Legal Aid system with even that of another Common Law system is an inexact process and potentially misleading. A wide range of factors – respective crime-rates, social inequalities, awareness of legal rights, the level of family breakdown, the quality of decision-making by public bodies (if decisions are made correctly there is little room for legal challenge), and the general cost of living – will dictate the overall budget in such a way as to make direct comparisons problematic.

The Labour Government did endeavour to ascertain the costs of legal practice from a criminal law point of view. In 1998, its plan to establish a Public Defender Service in England and Wales was announced in a White Paper entitled *Modernising Justice*. The Public Defender Service was eventually launched in May 2001 in a limited number of areas.

One of the aims of the Public Defender Service was to provide a form of benchmarking for the government as to (i) the quality of legal defence services being provided by private legal practice, and (ii) the cost of providing those services. Research into comparative costs in 2007 concluded that the average cost per case of the Public Defender Service (both in police station attendance and magistrates' courts proceedings) was in the region of 50% higher than that for a comparable private practice firms.[1] The implication is that the government had actually been receiving good value from its private firm Criminal Legal Aid providers. Going forward, however, it is likely that an enlarged Public Defender Service would be more directly vulnerable to cost-cutting pressures with the risk that processing cases cheaply may take priority over robust investigation and presentation of defences on behalf of accused persons.

Since 2010, the Coalition Government has pursued a general policy of seeking to control and often cut public spending in the wake of the banking and financial crisis, in which context the cost of providing Legal Aid has again become a concern. The increasing pressures on this budget culminated with the government issuing a Green Paper in 2010 with proposals for savings in the Legal Aid budget (essentially in the area of Civil Legal Aid) to the tune of £350 million by 2015.

This Green Paper and the ensuing consultation resulted in the passing of the Legal Aid, Sentencing and Punishment of Offenders Act 2012 (LASPO). This introduced changes in eligibility for Legal Aid with the intent of excluding all but the very poorest from being able to access such services. Even those on income-related benefits are no longer automatically entitled to receive Legal Aid. Further, there have also been changes to the amount of capital that an individual needs to own before being able to receive assistance.

Even more drastic were the changes to the types of civil cases that would qualify for Legal Aid assistance. These cuts "in scope" are wide ranging:

- Legal Aid for clinical negligence cases is now only available where a child has suffered neurological injury, resulting in them being severely disabled, during pregnancy, child birth or the eight week post-natal period.

- Legal Aid is now no longer available in the area of employment unless the matter involves a breach of the Equality Act 2010 or it arises in relation to the exploitation of an individual who is a victim of human trafficking.

- Legal Aid remains available for public law family cases (e.g. in care proceedings). However, it is generally only available for private family law cases (such as contact or divorce) if there is evidence of domestic violence or child abuse or in child abduction cases.

- Housing Law cases are now beyond the scope unless there is serious disrepair or homelessness, possession proceedings or for anti-social behaviour cases in the County Court.

- Debt cases are excluded unless there is an immediate risk to the debtor's home.

- Most immigration work is no longer covered by Legal Aid – except for persons in immigration detention or where torture is involved or in respect of claims arising under the Refugee Convention.

- Education cases are only covered in relation to Special Educational Needs.

- Welfare Benefit cases are also excluded except for appeals to the Upper Tribunal or higher courts.

Importantly, LASPO does allow for the Lord Chancellor to introduce new areas of law, and reintroduce old areas that have been removed back into the coverage of Legal Aid provision. Whether he or any future Lord Chancellor will do so, remains to be seen.

The Government itself has acknowledged that "Legal Aid recipients are amongst the most disadvantaged in society, reflecting both the nature of the problems they face as well as the eligibility rules for Legal Aid."[2] It has also admitted that the result of the LASPO "reforms" (perhaps, more accurately, "cuts") could lead to increased criminality and reduced social cohesion. Yet notwithstanding these admissions, notwithstanding opposition from almost all interested agencies, and notwithstanding a record numbers of defeats in the House of Lords, LASPO passed the Parliamentary process and came into effect on 1st April 2013.

the current position

In the spring of 2013, the Justice Secretary announced his intention to extract another £200 million plus of savings from the Legal Aid budget. A consultation paper on proposed further changes entitled *Transforming Legal Aid: delivering a more credible and efficient system* was issued in June 2013.

The changes mooted by this consultation were essentially fourfold in nature.

1. A further reduction in the scope of the matters covered by Civil Legal Aid (for example, in the area of prison law) and restrictions in judicial review cases;

2. Further reductions in payment rates for areas of Civil Legal Aid that remain in scope (for example, child care cases);

3. A restructuring of the Criminal Legal Aid market together with cuts in payment rates for both Solicitors and Barristers (notwithstanding that such rates had remained static – and sometimes fallen – for a number of years);

4. Further restrictions on those who will be eligible for advice and assistance even if they are eligible on financial grounds and their matter remains within scope; for example, the proposed introduction of a residence test for Civil Legal Aid claimants, so as to limit Legal Aid to those with a "strong connection" with the United Kingdom.

Writing in *The Solicitors' Journal* on 10th September 2013 in response to the government's further consultation on these changes, John Halford and Mike Schwarz said:

> Legal Aid is not a welfare benefit, it is an equalising measure. Its aim is to ensure that everyone subject to UK jurisdiction can enjoy their rights in a meaningful way through accessing legal advice when it would otherwise be unaffordable and representation funded to the extent necessary to ensure that the merits of any court case will determine the outcome, rather than the relative wealth or power of the opposing parties.
>
> These fundamental principles remain shamelessly compromised by the government's proposals… The crime proposals perpetuate a dangerous trend;

those for civil work will create a silenced minority whose cases will never be heard by our courts, regardless of their merits or what is at stake.

The proposals have been subject to a number of court challenges (for example, in respect of the proposed changes to criminal contract tendering and the evidence required in order to obtain Legal Aid in domestic violence cases) but, subject to being over-ruled by the courts, the government appears determined to proceed to implementation.

the likely cumulative effect of recent changes

The effect of successive governments' policies in the area of Legal Aid – and particularly those of recent times – will become increasingly apparent over the course of the coming months and years. What is already becoming visible is essentially similar to that forewarned by numerous stakeholders at the time of the various pre-implementation consultations.

The most visible result will be a decrease in the more traditional means of accessing legal services. A large proportion of Legal Aid advice and assistance has in the past been provided by firms of High Street Solicitors. The reduction in scope of matters qualifying for Legal Aid because of LASPO has resulted in many of those providers either closing their Family law and Housing law departments or dramatically reducing them in size. It will become more and more difficult for people to find a local solicitor, who they can meet with face to face, who is able to help them when they are in desperate need of legal advice and representation.

The voluntary advice sector will also suffer, however. The then Legal Services Commission (its successor is known as the Legal Aid Agency) had been funding a number of Community Legal Advice Centres (CLACS), originally designed to provide free legal advice and assistance principally in the area of social welfare law. These have all closed as a result of the recent funding cuts.

Law Centres are also severely affected. Many had the advantage of Civil Legal Aid contracts, contracts which are now more limited in size as a result of the implementation of LASPO. A number have already been forced to close or severely curtail the services that they are able to offer.

These are simply the initial and most visible effects of reform. However, beyond the possible 'business failures' and redundancies, there is a more fundamental issue – the impact on those in the greatest need of legal support. The major effect will undoubtedly be upon the consumer, the client, himself/herself. As mentioned above, a number of the legal issues that state funding would have been available for pre-LASPO have now been removed from scope. An individual unfortunate enough to be involved in such matters now needs to either (i) obtain funds in order to instruct a lawyer privately, (ii) represent in the matter, or (iii) 'grin and bear it' and leave the rights, claims, or problems unredressed.

Private funding will rarely be an option as the clients who would previously have qualified for Legal Aid are those with very limited resources. Some solicitors are trying to assist by 'unbundling' legal services, i.e. providing advice and assistance in respect of specific parts of, say, matrimonial proceedings rather than the whole. This may be of assistance to some litigants but is, at best, only a partial solution.

There is already a noticeable growth in people representing themselves in court proceedings as 'litigants in person'. Due to the complexity of the law this will often result in an inadequate presentation of their case, although a limited amount of assistance is available through the Personal Support Unit (PSU). The experience of the Family Court demonstrates that, as predicted, more judicial time/involvement is needed in such cases, resulting in increased costs within the court system itself. There also seems to be little doubt that an increased number of aggrieved persons will simply give up and walk away, with the sense of injustice and frustration that that brings.

> *There is already a noticeable growth in people representing themselves in court proceedings as 'litigants in person'. Due to the complexity of the law this will often result in an inadequate presentation of their case, although a limited amount of assistance is available through the Personal Support Unit (PSU).*

Concern is also being raised at the extremely low number of 'Exceptional Funding' grants of Legal Aid that have been granted by the Legal Aid Agency post the introduction of LASPO. Exceptional Funding grants were supposed to be a safety net that would catch clients in deserving matters that were otherwise outside of scope post 1st April 2013. The LASPO changes were sold to Parliament on the basis that such grants would be some form of panacea, with an estimate that around 6,000 of them would be available each year. However, as at 1st October 2014 fewer than 100 grants had been made. Legal practitioners have anecdotally said that administrative complexities and sometimes intransigence from the Legal Aid Agency have been the cause of difficulties. The situation here needs to be urgently reviewed.

Another issue that has arisen is in the area of Domestic Violence (DV). Legal Aid is still available in DV matters (subject to the normal financial eligibility criteria), but there are now much more stringent rules requiring the provision of evidence of domestic abuse before a Legal Aid application can be granted. The list of such evidence includes a letter from a GP, time spent in a refuge or proof that a place was needed but none was available.

Victims of domestic abuse often, however, fail to report the abuse that they have suffered due to shame or fear. Recent research carried out by Rights of Women, Women's Aid and Women's Aid Wales suggests that 43% of victims reported not having the prescribed documentation required to apply successfully for Legal Aid – meaning they could not even get to the first stage of meeting with a Solicitor.[3]

The net result is likely to be a vacuum so far as the provision of legal services is concerned. Solutions that have been suggested include an increased amount of pro bono legal provision, something akin to a partial technological solution with more advice and assistance being available on-line, and a simplification of legal processes. All would be welcomed and may assist to some extent. However, it must be emphasised that these are far from complete solutions. In particular, many people will still require face-to-face legal advice – the traditional way of delivering legal services. Legal problems tend by nature to relate to very individual circumstances.

Further, The Law Society, mindful of the ability of the Lord Chancellor, is currently collecting evidence of individual situations where the lack of Legal Aid has meant that needy and deserving individuals have been denied assistance. The campaign to redress the most serious effects of the recent changes continues, but realistically it would seem unlikely that the areas of law for which legal aid is available will be significantly widened.

government solutions?

Alert to the possible consequences of these reforms, the government has itself mooted certain possible solutions.

The government has assumed that British judges will be both prepared and able to deal with an increasing number of litigants in person, though it has not taken on board the extent to which judges dealing with litigants have to have a much greater 'hands on' investigative role. Where the parties' lawyers have not already sorted through the documents, marshalled the evidence and identified the best arguments, a judge's attempt to do so conscientiously will necessarily take up significant court time.

Part of the government's solution to this is to divert cases away from the courts. Mediation or out of court conciliation is now mandatory in many areas of law and must be considered in most others. Perhaps contrary to popular prejudice, mediation and conciliation processes tend to work well when lawyers are involved on both sides. When the parties go through mediation or conciliation without impartial advice and personal support, there is a risk that the outcomes merely repeat existing power differentials that caused the dispute in the first place or fail to stick because one side does not take the outcome seriously.

Another part of the government's solution is to suggest that lawyers should provide pro bono (i.e. free) legal advice to 'fill the gap' created by a reduction in Legal Aid provision. In the past, law firms doing Legal Aid work were able to provide a large amount of pro bono advice because they were sufficiently profitable. Moreover, they were local providers of legal advice and assistance, with local knowledge and local contacts. Often they had acted for the clients previously, meaning that they already had a fair amount of knowledge of their backgrounds and circumstances and had gained their trust. The problem is that, faced with less and less Legal Aid work and the reduction in real terms in the fees for that which remains, many such law firms are either closing their doors or reducing in size. The age of the family lawyer on every High Street may be over.

Another possible solution is found in the Legal Services Act 2007, which specifies as one of its regulatory objectives the need to improve access to justice. It also authorised the creation of new types of law firms known as Alternative Business Structures (ABSs), thereby allowing, for the first time in England and Wales, a degree of ownership of legal practices by non-lawyers. In granting licences for ABSs, the legal regulators must consider the regulatory objectives specified in the 2007 Act, including the possible adverse effect upon access to justice. There does appear to be a danger, however, of this being interpreted as a need to ensure the creation of newer legal services outlets in order to encourage competition within the legal services market. Whilst in the short term this might result in an increase in the number of legal services providers, the long-term result may well be that there are fewer, larger law firms, many, if not all, owned by non-lawyers. One only has to look at the fate of the building societies to see how changes in the law can lead, ultimately, to the creation of a few large institutions with less local roots.

New legal business structures/new entrants will be generally entering the market for profit motives rather than utilitarian or charitable ones. They will be primarily – if not purely – driven by the understandable need to return profit to their capital-introducing owners. There is therefore an obvious risk that the new entrants will "cream off" the more profitable work by targeting specific work categories, leaving more traditional law firms to carry out the less well-paid, more complex or more labour-intensive work. Such law firms as remain may be too stretched to be able to continue to offer pro bono or cheaper rate services. New entrants may choose to offer no such services at all.

conclusion

Access to justice is not a moral luxury, a nice-to-have just so long as it doesn't cost very much. The idea that everyone should be able to have their legal issues dealt with by the relevant court within a legal jurisdiction; that all should have access to good quality and appropriate legal advice and representation; and that neither cost nor social status nor any kind of disability should be a bar to accessing the courts, legal advice and representation is absolutely central to a just society.

In its *Access to Justice Review*, published in 2010, The Law Society of England and Wales, the professional body for solicitors, spelt out what this entailed, namely:

-   a respected judiciary of unimpeachable integrity;

-   a system of courts and tribunals which work efficiently to resolve disputes and adjudicate on civil and criminal cases at local and national levels;

-   a profession of lawyers with the competence and integrity to provide appropriate advice and representation to those who need it; and

-   the ability to access those lawyers and participate in the justice system without risk of financial ruin, taking into account the particular circumstances of the client.

According to the Law Society, "the system in England and Wales provides most of these characteristics but the last – the ability to participate in the justice system – causes the most difficulties." This should be a concern to all of us, but the fact that its burden is most likely to fall on those who can afford it least should be a matter of especial concern. According to former High Court judge Sir Mark Hedley:

> Frequently those involved in legal disputes, particularly in relation to family and criminal matters, are those who are the most disadvantaged and least well-equipped in society. For them, good quality legal representation in which they have confidence is a necessity. I have from time to time conducted serious cases with litigants in person and have been struck by the disadvantage at which so many of them find themselves. This is at its most marked where they are in effect resisting an institution of the state. Even in private proceedings however, one has readily observed serious inequalities where each side does not have a proper legal representation… It should therefore be the care of any reasonable society to ensure that those who are involved in such proceedings are able to enjoy an equality of arms which in my view is fundamental to the good administration of justice.

In a similar vein, Professor Dame Hazel Genn, Professor of Socio-Legal Studies at University College, London, has written that people who are socially excluded tend to experience more problems. A high proportion suffers multiple problems, which often appear in clusters or cascade into one another, one problem triggering others. Such problems – particularly if unresolved – can have a deleterious impact on people's lives, precipitating family breakdown, unemployment or loss of income, ill-health and disability, and there is significant anecdotal evidence of a link between unresolved legal problems and both poor health and crime.

> Evidence shows that low-income groups tend to suffer more problems than higher income groups and are less likely to do anything about them. Further, it seems that many people are not sure where to go or whom to approach to obtain resolution or redress and that there is a clear, significant unmet need for accessible and affordable sources of information and advice. Access to legal advice and assistance is necessary not only to lift up the socially excluded but also to prevent a slide into social exclusion in the first place.[4]

In some instances, the consequences of poor access to justice can be even more serious than just exacerbated social exclusion. It may be regarded as an extreme example, but there have been long-held concerns within the US justice system about the quality of some of the legal assistance provided in death penalty cases, as a result of the low fees paid to defence lawyers. It is considered that such levels of payment often result in a reduction in the quality of representation and/or unjust court verdicts where, for example, case documentation is not properly perused. In the words of Supreme Court Justice Ruth Bader Ginsburg,

> I have yet to see a death case among the dozens coming to the Supreme Court on eve-of-execution stay applications in which the defendant was well represented at trial. People who are well represented at trial do not get the death penalty.[5]

This is not a danger in England and Wales but the risks inherent in inadequate funding remain an issue and are increasingly likely to be so.

A purist would argue that defence costs in criminal trials should not be subject to state-imposed financial limitations at all, particularly bearing in mind that it is the state that will generally be the prosecuting authority. That is not, of course, a practical option when there are limited government resources. Funding must, however, be sufficient for there to be proper representation of those charged with criminal offences, particularly where the result of conviction would be loss of liberty or livelihood. Without it, there is an increased risk of serious injustice, and with each avoidable injustice our whole society is the poorer.

Two recent events have highlighted this. Firstly, in early 2014 a white collar fraud trial was stayed due to the inability of the defence to locate advocates prepared to work at reduced fee rates. In giving judgment, His Honour Judge Anthony Leonard QC said:

> It is the duty of the state to provide advocates at the required level of competence and experience pursuant to the court's interpretation of the government's own legislation. It is not for the defence to cut its just entitlement to representation to suit the state… the overriding objective of the Criminal Procedure Rules to deal with criminal trials justly is, therefore, subverted by failure of the state to provide adequate representation.[6]

Although the decision to stay the trial was overturned by the Court of Appeal, this was on the basis that the government had recruited additional lawyers to its Public Defence Service (discussed further above) who would be able to provide adequate representation to the defendants.

"A society's maturity and humanity will be measured by the degree of dignity it affords to the disaffected and the powerless."

Secondly, in a well-publicised case, Nigel Evans MP, a former Deputy Speaker of the House of Commons, was acquitted of serious sexual offences only to find that he could reclaim just a small proportion of his legal costs due to restrictions placed on the recoverability of legal costs by defendants – notwithstanding that they have been found to be innocent of any crimes alleged.[7]

The provision of access to justice for its citizens is a prime duty of government, a duty that extends – on a moral basis if nothing else – to those who, although not citizens of that particular nation state, are affected by that state's decisions or actions, such as asylum seekers or trafficked women. In the words of the Anglican priest, Paul Oestreicher, "a society's maturity and humanity will be measured by the degree of dignity it affords to the disaffected and the powerless."[8]

Of course, all governments face financial constraints, constraints that have been accentuated as a result of the 2008 banking crisis. However, all governments also make political choices as to where those limited financial resources are directed, and we believe that those choices recently made that pertain to the provision of access to justice require re-examination, for compelling practical, legal and ultimately moral reasons. If chapter 1 sought to set out a convincing reason why British Christians should see justice as a 'mission field', chapter 2 has tried to demonstrate how that field is not confined to those countries renowned for fragmentary or sub-standard legal systems but may increasingly include our own country. Chapter 3 concludes by outlining what this might mean in practice.

chapter 2 – references

1   Lee Bridges, Ed Cape, Paul Fenn, Anona Mitchell, Richard Moorhead and Avrom Sherr, *Evaluation of the Public Defender Service in England and Wales*, (Legal Services Commission, 2007), p .231.

2   Impact assessment issued by the UK Government, page 13, paragraph 39.

3   Mary O'Hara, 'Women will die – it's not too dramatic to say that', *The Guardian*, 10th September 2014.

4   The Law Society, *Access to Justice Review*, March 2010, Para 2.11–2.12; http://lawforlife.org.uk/wp-content/uploads/2013/05/law-society-access-to-justice-review-march-2010-246.pdf

5   Supreme Court Justice Ruth Bader Ginsburg, 9 April 2001; http://www.cbsnews.com/news/justice-backs-death-penalty-freeze/

6   HHJ Anthony Leonard QC in *R v Crawley*, Southwark Crown Court, 6 May 2015.

7   The state must not be deterred from bringing justified prosecutions by the prospect of having to pay unreasonably high legal costs to successful defendants, but it is also unjust that those who are innocent cannot recover a reasonable proportion of the cost of being represented by competent lawyers. A balance must be struck.

8   Paul Oestreicher, *Thirty Years of Human Rights* (The British Churches' Advisory Forum on Human Rights, 1980).

Christian concern for justice

Legal services in England and Wales are highly regarded worldwide. English law is one of our nation's greatest exports. Other countries are encouraged to use English expertise, to instruct English legal professionals, to make their commercial contracts subject to English law and to make the English jurisdiction their jurisdiction of choice, for the litigation of their disputes. The beneficial impact of this upon the economy of UK Plc is immense.

> *It will not reflect well upon our legal system if Russian oligarchs utilise our Commercial Court to settle their disputes but the average British citizen cannot afford or find anyone with the legal expertise to assist them with the threat of an eviction order.*

Underpinning all of this, however, is a pressing need to ensure that access to justice is maintained for our own citizens. It will not reflect well upon our legal system if Russian oligarchs utilise our Commercial Court to settle their disputes but the average British citizen cannot afford or find anyone with the legal expertise to assist them with the threat of an eviction order, in traumatic matrimonial proceedings, or in a complex personal injury claim.

It is a fact of our time that there appear to be fewer votes in the area of access to justice compared with, say, health services or education, but that should not diminish its importance and rightness. Access to justice is fundamental to the rule of law. The rule of law is a safeguard against arbitrary governance, whether by a totalitarian state or by mob rule. The rule of law obliges governments to act in accordance with written, publicly disclosed laws that have been passed and enforced in accordance with proper procedural steps ("due process"). It demands that there is equality before the law, that executive discretion is controlled, that the laws are reliably enforced by the courts, and that everyone is given a fair trial.

If, however, legal advice and representation is only available to those who can pay, the result will ultimately be that 'the powers that be' become above legal challenge. When accountability through the courts diminishes, the gap between the laws that exist on paper and the way things work in practice tends to increase. Both the rights of individual subjects and the common good are diminished. In order to establish the rule of law, it is not enough for the state to ensure that no-one is above the law; it must also ensure that no-one is below the law, that the protection of the law is accessible to all.

A government that seeks to serve those subject to its rule will therefore not shirk its responsibility to ensure that all have access to justice. Whilst there are political choices to be made about how this responsibility is to be discharged, it cannot be ignored, because access to justice is not a political tool with which to curry favour with the electorate. Rather, it is the prime responsibility of government.

This essay has been written from a perspective that some may not share and has made an argument some may not agree with. Both are occupational hazards of making a public case in a plural society. Different parties argue for different objectives on different grounds.

We have argued that the Christian scriptures – many of which are shared with Jews and respected by Muslims – emphasise four key points in relation to the exercise of justice:

(i)   justice must be administered impartially and equally;

(ii) access to justice should be universal rather than dependent on wealth or social status;

(iii) the implementation of impartial, equal and universal justice is threatened by economic imbalances and power differentials; and

(iv) advocacy is essential to the successful exercise of justice.

Wherever impartial, equal and universal justice, secured by effective and available advocacy, is under threat, the rule of law is undermined.

A focus upon the rights and liberties of others is one of the essential characteristics of the Christian faith. The Church has always done itself a disservice when that message is not the one that has been clearly transmitted to the outside world. The Christian Church should and does have an important voice when its concern is the public good and it speaks on behalf of those who are not able to buy the power or influence that can often dictate public policy.

But a Christian voice is only powerful when it is in partnership with Christian action. This essay has argued that we – meaning all people in the UK, and not just Christians – should recognise, appreciate and seek to protect access to justice in Britain today. The Christian concern for the voiceless can and should, however, extend beyond an intellectual appreciation of the problem. If Christians are serious about "seeking justice and defending the oppressed", they need to engage "hands on", and for that reason this essay ends with a challenge to the Church to respond practically to the growing need for legal advice, assistance and advocacy today.

It is important to recognise that many Christians are already involved in such work on an informal, ad hoc basis in their respective communities. A certain amount is most likely carried out by Christian lawyers in the back of church over an after service coffee and biscuit. Such individuals are liable to find themselves the go-to person in their congregation for casual legal advice. Unfortunately, due to its informal nature, this kind of work usually disappears under the radar, limiting both its visibility and the take-up of such assistance. In more recent years however, some have gone a step further than occasional person-to-person advice and have begun to introduce more structured initiatives in response to the ever growing need for affordable legal advice and assistance.

Peter Thompson, a retired barrister, has set up a church-based free legal advice service in the UK. Keen to give something back to his community in his retirement, Peter established St. James' Church Legal Advice Centre back in April 1998, at the invitation of the vicar and the Parish Church Council.[1] Lifting the burden of legal worry from members of his community and solving his neighbours' problems "with love" he perceives to be his clear "Christian duty". The Centre holds regular advice sessions three mornings a week at St. James' Church and Wilton Community Church and deals with a steady flow of work in the areas of housing, personal injury, family property, employment, immigration, social services, and social security. Contact is also available round the clock by telephone. Open to all, the centre assisted in over 400 cases last year.

Peter oversees all cases brought to the clinics, but is supported by a team of volunteers who assist with administration, conducting interviews and doing occasional research. All services provided are free of charge, although some choose to make a small donation to the church. The bulk of cases tend to be relatively easily solvable small claims and welfare problems, including personal injury claims, will-writing, boundary disputes, small business advice, and property disputes. More complex cases, where appropriate, are referred elsewhere for more specific, specialist advice.

Peter describes the Advice Centre's ethos as follows:

> We never turn anyone away. If the services needed are outside our competence (for example, conveyancing and court advocacy) we refer on to specialists; but most of the problems are ones which we can and do handle ourselves. Our mission is to lift the burden of legal worry from those who are oppressed by it. We give thanks for the opportunity to help our neighbours.[2]

In terms of structure, the Centre is connected interestingly to both the council-funded Legal Advice Providers Network,[3] which arranges free talks and training, and to the church, whose PCC makes recommendations based on an annual report. When asked to outline the practicalities of setting up this kind of church based legal assistance, Peter has mentioned the following considerations (and has also said he is willing to give advice to anyone considering setting up a church based Legal Advice Centre):

1. Utilise church premises/buildings as a resource;

2. Utilise young law students who need to gain legal experience;

3. Utilise retired individuals who have the skills, energy and time.

In reference to the cost, he said it should be reasonably self-financing, although Professional Indemnity Insurance (PII) is needed. It is worth noting that this is a very important and potentially expensive consideration and will need to be carefully considered. It should be particularly noted that PII matters are on a "claims made" basis, i.e. the relevant date is when knowledge of the mistake arises and not when the mistake was made. This may necessitate PII premiums having to be paid for some years after the closure of such a project.

Another potential difficulty is that professionals often feel unqualified to deal with issues which fall outside their area of expertise and therefore sometimes shy away from involvement in this kind of work. However, Peter Thompson insists that legal professionals should not be deterred by this and volunteers often do not necessarily need extensive legal training to deal with the majority of small claims brought to the clinics.

The St. James' Church Legal Advice Centre may have been the first Christian legal centre of this nature (as far as we can tell) but it is not the only one. More recently, the Salvation Army has opened a Housing Legal Advice Clinic in Ilford, Essex, teaming up with legal firm Sternberg Reed and the Refugee and Migrant Forum of East London. Statistics collected by law students concerning this centre found that housing was the most common concern for clients, followed by family issues and employment. For two thirds of clients this was the first official advice they had received on their issue.

For those Christians who *do* have extensive legal expertise to offer, setting up a fully-fledged, timing-consuming Legal Advice Centre is not the only way to get involved. A number of Christian lawyers have been involved in "pop-up" legal clinics at their local churches. These tend to work well and are a way of minimising risk, in particular if PII cover is provided as an extension of their own firms' insurance policy. An even easier and much less daunting way to help can be by volunteering for pre-existing community initiatives, such as not-for-profit secular Law Centres, Citizens Advice Bureaux or charities, who are always on the lookout for assistance, or even to provide financial assistance for such bodies.

Encouragingly, similar legal assistance initiatives are also being implemented in African countries. Organisations such as the Uganda Christian Lawyers Fraternity and the Rwandan Lawyers of Hope address issues of access to justice by providing education and by being present in the places where injustice might otherwise occur. They offer free legal education to the vulnerable, going into villages and prisons to teach people about their basic legal rights. They attend police stations and courts, where the simple fact that they are there as independent observers already raises standards. But more than that, they provide relational support to those who are often completely bewildered by the legal process which is happening. These organisations have impressively wide scope. In 2008-2009, for example, the UCLF reached over 37,000 people.[4]

Another example is BMS World Mission. BMS run short-term opportunities for selected Christian volunteers to Rwanda, Uganda and Kenya. Applications are welcomed from law students and young lawyers to spend a period of time assisting with community projects, participating in legal education seminars and conducting field research. In cultures devoid of any governmental legal support, the injection of such help into local organisations can assist in developing sustainable services. Although it is, of course, important to recognise the contrast in need here, such schemes provide an example of Christians becoming actively involved in providing legal advice and assistance on a voluntary (pro bono) basis to very needy communities.

One further example of Christians recognising this particular call of justice can be seen in the Salvation Army in Australia, which has established a full legal practice providing commercial and property law advice on a standard basis, the fees of which are used to fund a sister Legal Aid firm, Salvos Legal Humanitarian. Salvos Legal Humanitarian is a full service free law firm targeted at the marginalised in New South Wales and Queensland, providing advice on police matters, debt, neighbourhood disputes, family law, housing matters, and family migration and refugee matters.

In the UK, education, presence and debt advice are all combined in the approach of the charity Christians Against Poverty (CAP). Focussing on the issue of debt, CAP provides education by informing those who are in debt of the options available to them and by offering a money management course. CAP also has a network of local centres, each of which has volunteers who will befriend someone in debt and work with them through the process of getting control over their finances. The education and relational services that CAP offers are provided by local Christians, who receive training but do not need any specific legal qualifications or expertise. Legal advice is provided by a team of specialists at CAP's Head Office. CAP is therefore able to offer, from as low a cost base as possible, a wide range of services to those who are struggling with seemingly unmanageable debt.

Observing the success of CAP, could a similar model be applied to legal issues? An overarching Christian organisation may just provide the tools necessary for motivating individuals to get involved and offer up their skills to their communities. A support network of this nature, providing resources and training, could be the necessary formula for creating a cohesive Christian legal assistance system which allows for that focused delivery at local grassroots level. It could be just the tap on the back needed to get more Christians participating.

The picture in the USA shows that this is actually not an unprecedented system. In the US, the Christian Legal Society (CLS) presides over hundreds of smaller localised Christian legal assistance organisations across different regions, offering support, training and a sense of unity to the project.[5] The Society provides an educational grounding for Christian legal work in the USA and acts as the overarching body responsible for this work. They support 65 legal clinics in 28 states and 50 cities across the country run by CLS members and have ultimately succeeded in fostering an atmosphere in which it is easy to set up your own initiative and easy to do your bit. They emphasise the importance of the fact that these clinics are independently and locally run. It is local people that use the services and it therefore should be local people who run them; local people who are best equipped to be responsive and empathetic to the needs of their own communities.

The range of Christian legal services provided across individual States differ in formula, size and practice therefore. But they unite in mission. This mission is particularly well articulated in Bruce Strom's 2013 book *Gospel Justice*.[6] This offers advice and encouragement on how to set up legal projects in your own community through a series of case studies, and tracks the author's personal experience of hearing the call "to loose the chains of injustice… to set the oppressed free."[7]

Ultimately, however, the book "gives a face to our poor neighbour through the stories of real people."[8] The stories range from a deaf-mute mother being reunited with her estranged son, to a woman desperately working to cover her husband's health bills cheated by her employers, and are poignantly narrated alongside the parable of the Good Samaritan. "Today", Strom says, "the Samaritan could be a lawyer."[9] Like, Samaritans, lawyers are so "often distrusted and viewed as robbers with excessive fees."[10] On hearing the call to serve *his* neighbour, Bruce explains how he realigned his life, leaving his private sector legal firm to found Administer Justice,[11] a network of local Christian legal assistance programmes, which provided help to 30,000 clients in 2009.[12] This led him to the setting up of the national organisation, Gospel Justice Initiative,[13] which aims to "excite and equip churches, attorneys, and individuals to defend the rights of the poor and needy through legal help and gospel hope."[14]

There are, in reality, a number of different models that Christians could use in response to the increasing need to enable people to access justice, and not all of them demand legal knowledge. Many of the most vulnerable in our society need three things when operating in this area: they need someone to provide relational and emotional support as they deal with the trauma of injustice and of navigating the legal process; they need someone to help them tell their story, to get their story straight; and they need someone to give them legal advice. Almost all Christians can provide others with the kind of relational and emotional support involved in the first and second of these. Many people in churches know how to write letters, organise information and present arguments on behalf of others who are too distressed or who lack the education to be able to do so themselves. Christians can provide this support without needing any detailed knowledge of the law.

But there are also ways in which Christians can offer specifically legal advice. A church could run a pop-up legal clinic. Churches could set up legal advice networks or encourage their members to volunteer at local law centres or Citizens Advice Bureaux. A particular issue could be identified where injustice is likely to occur, such as family breakdown, debt, the minimum wage, housing or immigration, and develop the expertise to offer help on that issue. And finally, as CAP shows, there is a relatively low-cost 'semi-professional' model for helping people who face injustice through establishing a charity which uses local volunteers as much as possible to provide relational support and to collect and present information, but which has access to legal specialists as and when required.

This account has hopefully shown that there are many different ways in which Christians can get involved in providing legal advice, assistance and advocacy. But ultimately, whatever approach is adopted, the Christian community needs to recognise its responsibilities in respect of justice issues and to speak up for those who would not otherwise have a voice.

conclusion

Advocacy of this kind will not obviate the need to monitor and speak up about the wider political agenda concerning access to justice. It is notable, for example, that while changes introduced by successive governments have been ostensibly subjected to scrutiny in terms of their impact on human rights and equality,[15] such assessments have not expressly considered the impact of the proposed changes on access to justice, without which neither human rights nor equality can be secured. To this end, there is considerable merit in an independent access to justice impact assessment (which incorporates the existing human rights and equality assessments). The government will still have to make a political choice as to what action it decides to take following such an assessment, but the weight of such an assessment would remind the government of its over-riding obligation to provide a fair and affordable justice system for all those subject to its rule.

Scrutiny and responses of this kind are and will remain essential. Yet so, at the same time, is the grass-roots level activity. Christians believe that God can heal, and because of that, they built hospitals. Christians believe that God wants people to flourish, and because of that, they built schools. Christians believe that God wants justice, and because of that, they should be providing para-legal advice and support to people who are experiencing legal problems. There will always be a need to refer complex cases on to the professionals but justice is too important to be left in a vacuum.

A Church which takes seriously its responsibility to "speak up for those who cannot speak for themselves, for the rights of all who are destitute", and to "defend the rights of the poor and needy" will ensure that access to justice remains on the government's agenda. A legal profession will take seriously its collective responsibility to make legal services available in all cases where serious injustice will result if no-one speaks up. A people who are concerned about the rule of law and who believe that the protection of English law should extend to all within its territory will not take access to justice for granted. They will not accept a welfare state as a substitute for a just state nor accept a division between those who can afford to buy justice and those who cannot.

chapter 3 – references

1   http://www.st-james.org.uk/legal-advice-debt-management.php

2   Interview conducted with Lucinda Murphy, September 2014.

3   http://www.minutes.haringey.gov.uk/mgOutsideBodyDetails.aspx?ID=373

4   http://www.bmsworldmission.org/about-us/what-we-do/media-advocacy

5   http://www.christianlegalsociety.org/

6   http://gospeljusticebook.com/

7   Isaiah 58:6.

8   Bruce Strom, *Gospel Justice*, (Moody Publishers: Chicago, 2013), p. 25.

9   Ibid.

10   Ibid.

11   http://administerjustice.org/

12   Strom, *Gospel Justice*, p. 85.

13   https://www.gji.org/learn

14   Strom, *Gospel Justice*, p. 85.

15   See, for example, https://consult.justice.gov.uk/digital-communications/transforming-legal-aid